SYMPHONIC HYMNS FOR PIANO

7 SONOROUS ARRANGEMENTS BY PHILLIP KEVEREN

— PIANO LEVEL —
LATE INTERMEDIATE

Cover photo courtesy The Lyda Hills Texas Collection of Photographs
in Carol M. Highsmith's America Project,
Library of Congress, Prints & Photographs Division

ISBN 978-1-4950-9035-6

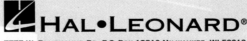

7777 W. BLUEMOUND RD. P.O. BOX 13819 MILWAUKEE, WI 53213

In Australia Contact:
Hal Leonard Australia Pty. Ltd.
4 Lentara Court
Cheltenham, Victoria, 3192 Australia
Email: ausadmin@halleonard.com.au

Visit Hal Leonard Online at
www.halleonard.com

Visit Phillip at
www.phillipkeveren.com

PREFACE

At this point in my writing career, I have arranged hymns in many, many styles and for myriad ensembles. It is a musical assignment of which I will never tire. I love the sturdy excellence and beauty of the Great Hymns.

When I begin the process of writing for orchestra, I often write a piano arrangement that serves as the template from which the orchestration blossoms. The voicings are created with various sections of the orchestra in mind – brass, strings, woodwinds, percussion, or combinations thereof. The arrangements in this collection were crafted from this point of view. So, the adjective "symphonic" refers to sound quality, not duration. I believe this to be a good thing if you are looking for an arrangement for a special moment in a church service – prelude, offertory, etc. I hope you find these settings to be nourishing but not long-winded.

BIOGRAPHY

Phillip Keveren, a multi-talented keyboard artist and composer, has composed original works in a variety of genres from piano solo to symphonic orchestra. Mr. Keveren gives frequent concerts and workshops for teachers and their students in the United States, Canada, Europe, and Asia. Mr. Keveren holds a B.M. in composition from California State University Northridge and a M.M. in composition from the University of Southern California.

CONTENTS

ALL CREATURES
OF OUR GOD AND KING

Words by FRANCIS OF ASSISI
Music from *Geistliche Kirchengesang*
Arranged by Phillip Keveren

With grandeur (♩ = 88)

ALL THINGS BRIGHT
AND BEAUTIFUL

Words by CECIL FRANCES ALEXANDER
17th Century English Melody
Arranged by Phillip Keveren

AT CALVARY

Words by WILLIAM R. NEWELL
Music by DANIEL B. TOWNER
Arranged by Phillip Keveren

GOD SO LOVED THE WORLD

from the oratorio *The Crucifixion*

Words from John 3:16, 17
Music by JOHN STAINER
Arranged by Phillip Keveren

CHRIST THE LORD IS RISEN TODAY

Words by CHARLES WESLEY
Music adapted from *Lyra Davidica*
Arranged by Phillip Keveren

With fanfare (♩ = 100)

THE CHURCH'S ONE FOUNDATION

Words by SAMUEL JOHN STONE
Music by SAMUEL SEBASTIAN WESLEY
Arranged by Phillip Keveren

FOR THE BEAUTY OF THE EARTH

Words by FOLLIOT S. PIERPOINT
Music by CONRAD KOCHER
Arranged by Phillip Keveren

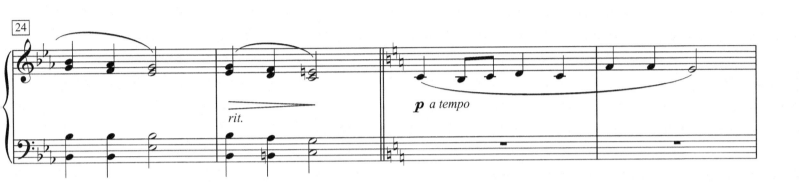

HE HIDETH MY SOUL

Inspired by Dvořák's Symphony No. 9 ("From the New World")

Words by FANNY J. CROSBY
Music by WILLIAM J. KIRKPATRICK
Arranged by Phillip Keveren

HIS EYE IS ON THE SPARROW

Words by CIVILLA D. MARTIN
Music by CHARLES H. GABRIEL
Arranged by Phillip Keveren

24

I NEED THEE EVERY HOUR

Inspired by Tchaikovsky's Symphony No. 5 (Third Movement "Waltz")

Words by ANNIE S. HAWKS
Music by ROBERT LOWRY
Arranged by Phillip Keveren

JESUS LOVES EVEN ME
(I Am So Glad)

Words and Music by
PHILIP P. BLISS
Arranged by Phillip Keveren

LIVING FOR JESUS

Words by THOMAS O. CHISHOLM
Music by C. HAROLD LOWDEN
Arranged by Phillip Keveren

REJOICE, THE LORD IS KING

Inspired by Mozart's Symphony No. 41 ("Jupiter")

Words by CHARLES WESLEY
Music by JOHN DARWALL
Arranged by Phillip Keveren

NOW THANK WE ALL OUR GOD

Inspired by Haydn's Symphony No. 94 ("Surprise")

German words by MARTIN RINKART
English Translation by CATHERINE WINKWORTH
Music by JOHANN CRÜGER
Arranged by Phillip Keveren

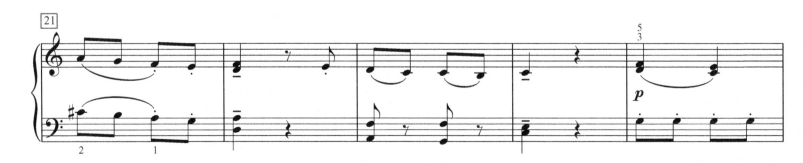

ONCE TO EVERY MAN AND NATION

Inspired by Beethoven's Symphony No. 7

Words by JAMES RUSSELL LOWELL
Music by THOMAS J. WILLIAMS
Arranged by Phillip Keveren

Solemnly (♩ = 60)

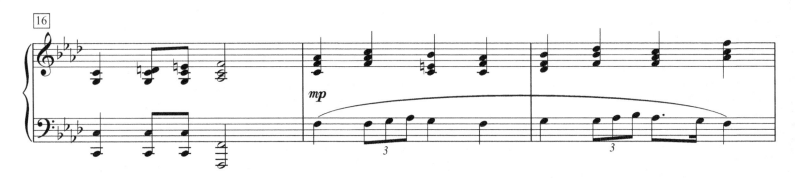

TELL ME THE STORIES OF JESUS

Inspired by Smetana's tone poem *The Moldau*

Words by WILLIAM H. PARKER
Music by FREDERIC A. CHALLINOR
Arranged by Phillip Keveren

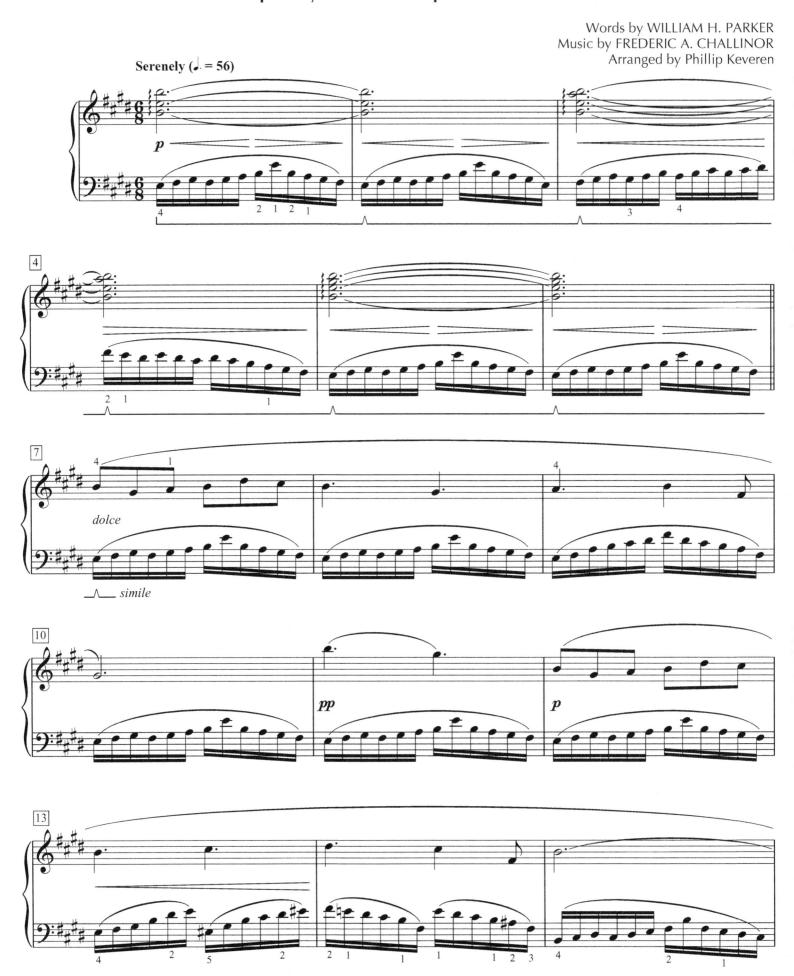

WE'VE A STORY TO TELL TO THE NATIONS

Inspired by Beethoven's *The Consecration of the House Overture*

Words and Music by
H. ERNEST NICHOL
Arranged by Phillip Keveren

THE PHILLIP KEVEREN SERIES

PIANO SOLO

ABBA FOR CLASSICAL PIANO
00156644.................................$14.99

ABOVE ALL
00311024.................................$11.95

AMERICANA
00311348.................................$10.95

THE BEATLES
00306412.................................$14.99

THE BEATLES FOR CLASSICAL PIANO
00312189.................................$14.99

BEST PIANO SOLOS
00312546.................................$14.99

BLESSINGS
00156601.................................$12.99

BROADWAY'S BEST
00310669.................................$12.95

CANZONE ITALIANA
00312106.................................$12.99

A CELTIC CHRISTMAS
00310629.................................$12.99

THE CELTIC COLLECTION
00310549.................................$12.95

CHRISTMAS MEDLEYS
00311414.................................$12.99

CHRISTMAS AT THE MOVIES
00312190.................................$12.99

CHRISTMAS WORSHIP MEDLEYS
00311769.................................$12.99

CINEMA CLASSICS
00310607.................................$12.95

CLASSIC WEDDING SONGS
00311101.................................$10.95

CLASSICAL FOLK
00311292.................................$10.95

CLASSICAL JAZZ
00311083.................................$12.95

COLDPLAY FOR CLASSICAL PIANO
00137779.................................$14.99

CONTEMPORARY WEDDING SONGS
00311103.................................$12.99

DISNEY SONGS FOR CLASSICAL PIANO
00311754.................................$14.99

FAVORITE WEDDING SONGS
00311881.................................$12.99

FIDDLIN' AT THE PIANO
00315974.................................$12.99

THE FILM SCORE COLLECTION
00311811.................................$12.99

GOSPEL GREATS
00144351.................................$12.99

THE GREAT MELODIES
00312084.................................$12.99

GREAT STANDARDS
00311157.................................$12.95

THE HYMN COLLECTION
00311071.................................$12.99

HYMN MEDLEYS
00311349.................................$12.99

HYMNS WITH A TOUCH OF JAZZ
00311249.................................$12.99

I COULD SING OF YOUR LOVE FOREVER
00310905.................................$12.95

JINGLE JAZZ
00310762.................................$14.99

BILLY JOEL FOR CLASSICAL PIANO
00175310.................................$14.99

ELTON JOHN FOR CLASSICAL PIANO
00126449.................................$14.99

LET FREEDOM RING!
00310839.................................$9.95

ANDREW LLOYD WEBBER
00313227.................................$14.95

MANCINI MAGIC
00313523.................................$12.99

MORE DISNEY SONGS FOR CLASSICAL PIANO
00312113.................................$15.99

MOTOWN HITS
00311295.................................$12.95

PIAZZOLLA TANGOS
00306870.................................$14.99

QUEEN FOR CLASSICAL PIANO
00156445.................................$3.99

RICHARD RODGERS CLASSICS
00310755.................................$12.95

SHOUT TO THE LORD!
00310699.................................$12.95

THE SOUND OF MUSIC
00119403.................................$14.99

THE SPIRITUALS COLLECTION
00311978.................................$10.99

TREASURED HYMNS FOR CLASSICAL PIANO
00312112.................................$14.99

THE TWELVE KEYS OF CHRISTMAS
00144926.................................$12.99

WORSHIP WITH A TOUCH OF JAZZ
00294036.................................$12.99

YULETIDE JAZZ
00311911.................................$17.99

EASY PIANO

AFRICAN-AMERICAN SPIRITUALS
00310610.................................$10.99

CELTIC DREAMS
00310973.................................$10.95

CHRISTMAS POPS
00311126.................................$14.99

CLASSIC POP/ROCK HITS
00311548.................................$12.95

A CLASSICAL CHRISTMAS
00310769.................................$10.95

CLASSICAL MOVIE THEMES
00310975.................................$10.99

CONTEMPORARY WORSHIP FAVORITES
00311805.................................$14.99

DISNEY SONGS FOR EASY CLASSICAL PIANO
00144352.................................$12.99

EARLY ROCK 'N' ROLL
00311093.................................$10.99

EASY WORSHIP MEDLEYS
00311997.................................$12.99

FOLKSONGS FOR EASY CLASSICAL PIANO
00160297.................................$12.99

GEORGE GERSHWIN CLASSICS
00110374.................................$12.99

GOSPEL TREASURES
00310805.................................$12.99

THE VINCE GUARALDI COLLECTION
00306821.................................$14.99

HYMNS FOR EASY CLASSICAL PIANO
00160294.................................$12.99

IMMORTAL HYMNS
00310798.................................$10.95

JAZZ STANDARDS
00311294.................................$12.99

LOVE SONGS
00310744.................................$10.95

POP BALLADS
00220036.................................$12.95

POP GEMS OF THE '50s
00311406.................................$12.95

A RAGTIME CHRISTMAS
00102887.................................$10.99

RAGTIME CLASSICS
00311293.................................$10.95

SANTA SWINGS
00312028.................................$12.99

SONGS OF INSPIRATION
00103258.................................$12.99

SWEET LAND OF LIBERTY
00310840.................................$10.99

TIMELESS PRAISE
00310712.................................$12.95

10,000 REASONS
00126450.................................$14.99

TV THEMES
00311086.................................$10.95

21 GREAT CLASSICS
00310717.................................$12.99

WEEKLY WORSHIP
00145342.................................$16.99

BIG-NOTE PIANO

CHILDREN'S FAVORITE MOVIE SONGS
00310838.................................$10.95

CHRISTMAS MUSIC
00311247.................................$10.95

CONTEMPORARY HITS
00310907.................................$12.99

HOLIDAY FAVORITES
00311335.................................$12.95

HOW GREAT IS OUR GOD
00311402.................................$12.95

INTERNATIONAL FOLKSONGS
00311830.................................$12.99

JOY TO THE WORLD
00310888.................................$10.95

THE NUTCRACKER
00310908.................................$10.99

BEGINNING PIANO SOLOS

AWESOME GOD
00311202.................................$10.95

CHRISTIAN CHILDREN'S FAVORITES
00310837.................................$12.99

CHRISTMAS FAVORITES
00311246.................................$10.95

CHRISTMAS TIME IS HERE
00311334.................................$12.99

CHRISTMAS TRADITIONS
00311117.................................$10.99

EASY HYMNS
00311250.................................$10.99

EVERLASTING GOD
00102710.................................$10.99

JAZZY TUNES
00311403.................................$10.95

KIDS' FAVORITES
00310822.................................$10.95

PIANO DUET

CLASSICAL THEME DUETS
00311350.................................$10.99

HYMN DUETS
00311544.................................$10.95

PRAISE & WORSHIP DUETS
00311203.................................$11.95

STAR WARS
00119405.................................$14.99

HAL•LEONARD®

www.halleonard.com

*Prices, contents, and availability
subject to change without notice.*